First World War
and Army of Occupation
War Diary
France, Belgium and Germany

51 DIVISION
154 Infantry Brigade
Lancashire Fusiliers
2/5th Battalion
1 May 1915 - 31 October 1915

WO95/2887/3

The Naval & Military Press Ltd
www.nmarchive.com
Published in association with The National Archives

Published by

The Naval & Military Press Ltd

Unit 10 Ridgewood Industrial Park,

Uckfield, East Sussex,

TN22 5QE England

Tel: +44 (0) 1825 749494

www.naval-military-press.com

www.nmarchive.com

This diary has been reprinted in facsimile from the original. Any imperfections are inevitably reproduced and the quality may fall short of modern type and cartographic standards.

© **Crown Copyright**
Images reproduced by permission of The National Archives, London, England, 2015.

Contents

Document type	Place/Title	Date From	Date To
Heading	WO95/2887/3 2/5 Battalion Lancashire Fusiliers		
Heading	51st Division 154th Infy Bde 2-5th Bn Lancashire Fusrs 1915 May-Dec 1915		
Heading	51st Division 2/5th Lancashire Vol I From 1st To 31st May 1915		
War Diary	Bedford	01/05/1915	02/05/1915
War Diary	Southampton	02/05/1915	02/05/1915
War Diary	Havre	03/05/1915	03/05/1915
War Diary	Bedford	03/05/1915	03/05/1915
War Diary	Folkestone	03/05/1915	03/05/1915
War Diary	Boulogne	04/05/1915	04/05/1915
War Diary	Havre	04/05/1915	04/05/1915
War Diary	Pont. De Briques	04/05/1915	04/05/1915
War Diary	Berguettes	05/05/1915	05/05/1915
War Diary	Norrent Fontes	06/05/1915	06/05/1915
War Diary	Calonne Sur La Lys	07/05/1915	15/05/1915
War Diary	Merris	16/05/1915	18/05/1915
War Diary	La Gorgue	19/05/1915	19/05/1915
War Diary	Wallon Cappel	19/05/1915	20/05/1915
War Diary	Arques	21/05/1915	31/05/1915
Heading	51st Division 2/5th Lancashire Front Vol II From 1st To 30th June 1915		
War Diary	Arques	01/06/1915	30/06/1915
Heading	51st Division 2/5th Lancashire Fus Vol III From 1st To 31st July 1915		
War Diary	Arques	01/07/1915	08/07/1915
War Diary	La Gorgue	09/07/1915	09/07/1915
War Diary	Lavantie	10/07/1915	23/07/1915
War Diary	Merville	24/07/1915	27/07/1915
War Diary	La Gorgue	28/07/1915	28/07/1915
War Diary	Corbie	29/07/1915	30/07/1915
War Diary	Albert	31/07/1915	31/07/1915
Heading	51st Division 2/5th Lancashire Fusrs Vol IV From 1st To 31st Aug 1915		
War Diary	Bois d'Authville	01/08/1915	07/08/1915
War Diary	Martinsart	08/08/1915	12/08/1915
War Diary	Senlis	13/08/1915	28/08/1915
War Diary	Aveluy	29/08/1915	31/08/1915
Heading	51st Division 2/5th Lancashire Fusrs Vol V Sep 1.15		
Heading	War Diary Of 2/5th Batt. Lancashire Fusiliers From September 1. To September 30 (Volume 1)		
War Diary	Aveluy	01/09/1915	05/09/1915
War Diary	Martinsart	06/09/1915	10/09/1915
War Diary	Post Lesdos Authille	11/09/1915	21/09/1915
War Diary	Senlis	22/09/1915	26/09/1915
War Diary	Aveluy	27/09/1915	30/09/1915
Heading	51st Division 2/5th Lancs Fus Oct 1915 Vol VI		
Heading	War Diary 2/5 Of Batt Lancashire Fusillers From October 31 1915 To October 31 1915 Volume 1		
War Diary	Aveluy	01/10/1915	14/10/1915

War Diary	Post Lesdos	15/10/1915	20/10/1915
War Diary	Lesdos	21/10/1915	26/10/1915
War Diary	Aveluy	27/10/1915	31/10/1915

WO 95/2887/3
2/5 Battalion Lancashire Fusiliers

51ST DIVISION
154TH INFY BDE

2-5TH BN LANCASHIRE FUSRS
MAY-DEC 1915

To 55 DIV
164 BDE

51st Division

13/6443

154/51

2/5th Lancashire Fus^rs

Vol I

From 1st to 31st May 1915

Caudell I.H.
6 sheets

WAR DIARY of 2nd/5th LANCASHIRE FUSILIERS.

Army Form C. 2118.

WAR DIARY
or
INTELLIGENCE SUMMARY.
(Erase heading not required.)

Instructions regarding War Diaries and Intelligence Summaries are contained in F. S. Regs., Part II. and the Staff Manual respectively. Title pages will be prepared in manuscript.

Place	Date	Hour	Summary of Events and Information	Remarks and references to Appendices
BEDFORD	1.5.15	Midnight	Transport and Machine Gun Section entrained for SOUTHAMPTON. MAJOR H. N. MILNES in command, with LIEUT. W. ABBOTTS (Transport Officer) and LIEUT. C. W. B. HILL (Machine Gun Officer) and 101 other ranks.	JMB.
do	2.5.15	—	Engaged in preparations for departure of Battalion.	JMB.
SOUTHAMPTON	do	4 p.m.	Transport etc (as set out above) sailed for HAVRE.	
HAVRE	3.5.15	2 a.m.	Transport disembarked, and went into rest camp.	
BEDFORD	do	4:30 p.m.	Personnel of Battalion entrained for FOLKESTONE. 8 & 28 officers. 840 other ranks (20 N.C.O.s/men left behind in hospital)	
FOLKESTONE	do	10:30 p.m.	Detrained at FOLKESTONE. Entrained for BOULOGNE.	JMB.
		11:30 p.m.	Sailed. Interpolar statier.	
BOULOGNE	4.5.15	12:30 a.m.	Disembarked and rested at ST. MARTIN'S Camp.	
HAVRE		2:30 a.m.	Transport disembarked left by train for PONT. DE BRIQUES, near BOULOGNE.	
PONT. DE BRIQUES		5:30 p.m.	Battalion and Transport left by train. 3 N.C.O.s & men to Hospital sick.	
		Midnight	Detrained at BERGUETTES	JMB.
BERGUETTES	5.5.15	1 a.m.	Marched out. 1 man left behind – injured.	
AIRE ENT		3 a.m.	Went into billets, which were from, and rested. 1 man to Base Hospital. 1 man returned to duty.	JMB
FONTES	6.5.15	8:30 p.m.	Marched out after resting all day. Roads very heavy, and Brigade moved very slowly. 11 N.C.O.s/men left behind sick. 1 man to England.	JMB.

WAR DIARY or INTELLIGENCE SUMMARY

Army Form C. 2118.

Place	Date	Hour	Summary of Events and Information	Remarks and references to Appendices
CALONNE SUR LA LYS	7.5.15	3.a.m.	Arrived and went into billets, in the West (ST. FLORIS) side. Rested during day. 1 man to England	JWB.
	8.5.15	—	Telephonic communication established between companies and Batt. H-Q. Company Parades during the day. 1 man to England - sick.	JWB.
	9.5.15	—	Company training. do	JWB.
	10.5.15	—	do 2/Lt. J.B. PACKMAN to England - sick.	JWB.
	11.5.15	—	Battalion inspected by Companies by Brig BRIGADIER-GEN. HIBBERT, commanding 154th Infantry Brigade	JWB.
	12.5.15	—	Company Parades.	JWB.
	13.5.15	—	do	JWB.
	14.5.15	—	do	JWB.
	15.5.15	9.30am	9 NCO & 7 men left billets - sick. Marched out via CALONNE, + MERVILLE. Roads bad, and some rain falling.	
MERRIS	do	2.0 pm	Arrived, and went into billets. All farms, taken over from KING EDWARD'S HORSE.	JWB.
	16.5.15	—	Company & Battalion Parades. 11 NCOs & men to Field Ambulance.	JWB.
	17.5.15	—	do 2 do do returned to duty. 6 men to Field Ambulance. 1 man to F.A.	JWB.
	18.5.15	9 p.m.	Marched out via NEUF BERQUIN. — Roads bad, some rain falling, but warm.	JWB.
LA GORGUE	19.5.15	5 am	Arrived and Went into billets. Cloth mills and farms.	JWB.

WAR DIARY
or
INTELLIGENCE SUMMARY.
(Erase heading not required.)

Army Form C. 2118.

Instructions regarding War Diaries and Intelligence Summaries are contained in F. S. Regs., Part II. and the Staff Manual respectively. Title pages will be prepared in manuscript.

Place	Date	Hour	Summary of Events and Information	Remarks and references to Appendices
LA GORGUE	19.5.15	10.30 a.m.	Marched out via HAZEBROUCK, after very short rest. Roads pretty good, but men tired & owing to previous days on night's march. Weather condition - very hot.	JMB.
WALLON- CAPPEL	do	4 p.m.	Marched in, and billeted in farms. Very good billets.	JMB.
	20.5.15	1.30 p.m.	Marched due West to ARQUES. Very hot.	JMB.
		3 p.m.	Inspected on the march by GENERAL STOPFORD, commanding H-Q Troops.	JMB.
ARQUES		3.30 p.m.	Marched in. Billeted in trams.	JMB.
	21.5.15		Rested. Lion Staff Sgt. 1167 W. Wray 3rd Bit. Co. A.O.C. attached.	JMB.
	22.5.15		Began training under GENERAL STOPFORD, MAJOR NEEDHAM, and MAJOR EDEN. 3 A.S.c. N.co's been attached.	JMB.
	23.5.15		Training.	JMB.
	24.5.15		do	JMB.
	25.5.15		do	JMB.
	26.5.15		do 2 N.C.O's to MALASSINE Hospital.	JMB.
	27.5.15		do	JMB.
	28.5.15		do	JMB.

Army Form C. 2118.

WAR DIARY
or
INTELLIGENCE SUMMARY.
(Erase heading not required.)

Instructions regarding War Diaries and Intelligence Summaries are contained in F.S. Regs., Part II. and the Staff Manual respectively. Title pages will be prepared in manuscript.

Place	Date	Hour	Summary of Events and Information	Remarks and references to Appendices
ARQUES.	29.5.15	—	Training. 4 men returned from hospital.	AM3.
	30.5.15	—	Rest.	JM3.
	31.5.15	—	Training.	JM3.

1577 Wt.W10791/1773 500,000 1/15 D. D. & L. A.D.S.S./Forms/C. 2118.

51st Division

121/6443

2/5th Lancashire Fus.

Vol II

From 1st to 30th June 1915

WAR DIARY of 2nd/5th LANCASHIRE FUSILIERS

Army Form C. 2118.

INTELLIGENCE SUMMARY

(Erase heading not required.)

Place	Date	Hour	Summary of Events and Information	Remarks and references to Appendices
ARQUES.	1.6.15.		Training. 3 N.C.O's & men returned to duty from hospital. 2 men previously reported to England still in hospital in France. 2 men to hospital. Strength 30 officers 943 other ranks, 40 of whom are in hospitals in France.	A.M.3.
do	2.6.15		Training.	A.M.3.
	3.6.15		do	A.M.3.
	4.6.15		do "A" Coy at WISQUES for instruction in trench digging. 1 man returned from hospital.	A.M.3.
	5.6.15.		do. Rest, and Church Parade.	A.M.3.
	6.6.15.		Training.	A.M.3.
	7.6.15		Range at RUE. ST. VAUBAN at disposal of "A" Coy. 4 N.C.O's & men to England.	A.M.3.
	8.6.15.		Training.	A.M.3.
	9.6.15.		Lieut-Col. J. HALL returned to England. MAJOR M.J. SHIRLEY of the ARTIST RIFLES takes command of the Battalion. Training.	A.M.3.
	10.6.15		Training. "D" Coy to use range at ST. OMER. 3 N.C.O's & men discharged from hospital. CAPT. J.E. JEFFREYS. arrived for duty as Adjutant (vice CAPT. J.J.P. CUMMINS.) from 1/1st D.L.I.	A.M.3.
	11.6.15		Training.	A.M.3.

WAR DIARY
or
INTELLIGENCE SUMMARY.
(Erase heading not required.)

Army Form C. 2118.

Place	Date	Hour	Summary of Events and Information	Remarks and references to Appendices
ARQUES	12.6.15		Training. 1 man 6th D.L.I. attached. 2 N.C.O's returned to duty.	AWB
	13.6.15.		1 man 1st D.L.I. attached. Route march.	AWB
	14.6.15		Route march.	AWB
	15.6.15		"B" Coy using range. Remainder training.	AWB
	16.6.15		Training.	AWB
	17.6.15.		Training. All acting ranks made substantive for duration of War.	AWB
	18.6.15.		Training. 1 N.C.O & 40 men returned to Base.	AWB
	19.6.15		Training.	AWB
	20.6.15.		Rest.	AWB
	21.6.15		Training. 1 man died in Hospital.	AWB
	22.6.15		Route march. Battalion inspected by GEN. STOPFORD.	AWB
	23.6.15		Training. CAPT J.W. JEFFREYS (Adjutant) went on leave.	AWB
	24.6.15		do. 2/LT N.L. KEMP appointed Bomb Officer to Battalion.	AWB
	25.6.15.		do. 2 R.E., 2 A.S.C., 1 Sth. Wales Bord., 7 London Rifle Brig., attached for rations only as and from 15.6.15.	AWB
	26.6.15		do.	AWO

Army Form C. 2118.

WAR DIARY
or
INTELLIGENCE SUMMARY.
(Erase heading not required.)

Instructions regarding War Diaries and Intelligence Summaries are contained in F. S. Regs., Part II. and the Staff Manual respectively. Title pages will be prepared in manuscript.

Place	Date	Hour	Summary of Events and Information	Remarks and references to Appendices
ARQUES.	27.6.15		Training.	
	28.6.15		do. 17 N.C.O's given to England.	AWB
	29.6.15		do. Football match v. ARTIST'S RIFLES at ST. OMER.	AWB
	30.6.15		do. Field Operations. 2.A.S.C. returned to unit. CAPT. J.W. JEFFREYS returned from leave.	AWB

121/6443

51st Division

2/5th Lancashire Fus'

Vol III

From 1st to 31st July 1915

S.H.
5 sheets

WAR DIARY of 2nd/5th LANCASHIRE FUSILIERS.

INTELLIGENCE SUMMARY

Army Form C. 2118.

Instructions regarding War Diaries and Intelligence Summaries are contained in F. S. Regs., Part II. and the Staff Manual respectively. Title pages will be prepared in manuscript.

Place	Date	Hour	Summary of Events and Information	Remarks and references to Appendices
ARQUES.	1.7.15	—	Training	JWB
	2.7.15	—	do. 4 men to England.	JWB
	3.7.15.	—	do.	JWB
	4.7.15	—	do.	JWB
	5.7.15	—	do. 12 men of other units attached for return only 15.6.15 struck off. Today	JWB
	6.7.15	—	do. Orders to move on the 8th to join the 154th Brigade.	JWB
	7.7.15	4.30 p.m.	Transport left for AIRE en route for LA GORGUE, accompanied by Lt ABBOTTS & Lt & Q.M. J BOWD.	JWB
	8.7.15	11.30 a.m.	Battalion left Market Square in 44 motor omnibuses, travelled via AIRES, ST. VENANT, MERVILLE, to LA GORGUE. Billeted in a cloth mill. Strength 29 officers and 887 NCO's & men. Came under command of BRIGr GENl HIBBERT. BRIGADE-MAJOR – MAJOR BRUCE, 4/1st PIONEERS. IND. ARMY. IN-co to M-G School at WISQUES.	JWB
LA GORGUE	9.7.15	3.30 PM	Moved to billets along RUE DU BACQUEROT, LAVANTIE. For12 13 T/6 occupied by "X" Company and one M-G. The other M-G pushed up to within 50 yds of first-line trenches. 1 man to England.	JWB
LAVANTIE.	10.7.15	5.0.PM	Moved back to a point 1 mile E. of la Gorgue. 1 man wounded by rifle bullet.	JWB
	11.7.15	9.0.PM	150 men "X" Company slipping into an outpost line. Returned 3 a.m. the 12th	JWB
	12.7.15		10 officers & 30 other ranks went to trenches held by 1/5th K.L.R. for experience in trench warfare.	JWB

Army Form C. 2118.

WAR DIARY
or
INTELLIGENCE SUMMARY.
(Erase heading not required.)

Place	Date	Hour	Summary of Events and Information	Remarks and references to Appendices
LAVANTIE.	13.7.15		5 men from Hospital, 3 returned from Base. 1 man wounded. 2 men to England. 3001 Pte T. Whilton sentenced to 112 days Hard labour by F.G.C.M. Brown, Major MILNES.	
	14.7.15	9 P.M.	Held at ARQUES 7.7.15. "Stealing goods the property of a comrade". L⁺ C.W.B. HILL shot through head in the 17 Communication Trench on return from visit to trenches for instructional purposes. Relieved during night. Working party of 150 men & 2 officers working on support lines in spite of heavy rain till 3 a.m.	2/M.B.
	15.7.15	4 P.M.	Took over Trenches from 1/8 K.L.R. and 1/1 Scot. Rifles. Moat point to German 120 yds at RED LAMP CORNER.	3/M.B.
	16.7.15	1 P.M.	Trenches one of breastworks only, opposite AUBERS. If digging is resorted to trench fills with water. Loud movements of German transport opposite our right. Brought by his army. No result.	
	16.7.15	night	One man of Z Coy went mad. Whilst agreeing to bring him to dressing station 1 man of 1/8 K.L.R. killed. CAPT. RAMSDEN to Hospital sick (15/7/15). 1 killed, 3 wounded, 7 to hospital sick. 1 N.C.O. from hospital. 2/LT. WATERHOUSE opposite Loophole Officer.	4/M.B.
	17.7.15		Quiet day & night. 4 men wounded.	5/M.B.
	18.7.15		Quiet day & night. 2 men wounded.	6/M.B.
	19.7.15	7.45 P.M.	Quiet all day, but 7.45 P.M. Germans shelled our trenches with 6" Howitzers. Four trenches in front, and much damage done to shelters and parapets. One line and 2 comms alleyway was followed by Germans coming out, but they were sent back by rifle & M-G fire. Communication cut off at outbreak of Tephine shelling, but wires were repaired under fire inside ten minutes. By 9.15 P.M. all was quiet. 1 man killed.	
	20.7.15		11 wounded. 4 wounded slightly. 1 accidentally wounded. 1 man to Hospital sick. Quiet day. Trenches repaired during previous night. Rations brought up by pack mules to a point 800 yds from trenches. 2 men wounded. 1 slight 11 sick to hospital.	7/M.B. 8/M.B.

1577 Wt.W1075 1/773 500,000 1/15 D.D.&L. A.D.S.S./Forms/C. 2118.

Army Form C. 2118.

WAR DIARY
OR
INTELLIGENCE SUMMARY.
(Erase heading not required.)

Instructions regarding War Diaries and Intelligence Summaries are contained in F. S. Regs., Part II. and the Staff Manual respectively. Title pages will be prepared in manuscript.

Place	Date	Hour	Summary of Events and Information	Remarks and references to Appendices
LAVANTIE	21.7.15	6 p.m.	Sharp burst of rifle fire from Germans on our right. Otherwise quiet. 2 men wounded. 1 to Hospital	JWB.
	22.7.15		Gun spoke on 19th inst. 3 to Hospital sick. Lt. R.W. KIRKMAN to Hospital sick. 5 men returned from Hospital	
			CAPT. E.R. RAMSDEN to England sick. 7 men to England. 4 men to Hospital sick & 2 men wounded.	
	22.7.15		G.O. of 2nd A.T.S.H. visits trenches prior to taking over. 1 N.C.O. killed. 1 Wounded. 2 to Hospital sick	JWB.
			1 man returned from Hospital. Quiet day.	
	23.7.15	9 p.m.	Relieved by 2nd A.T.S.H. Much rain. Trenches slippy. Tea & potatoes before arriving in billets	JWB.
			between MERVILLE & EST AIRES.	
MERVILLE	24.7.15		Billets rather cramped but good.	JWB.
	25.7.15		3 men returned to Bn. MAJOR SHIRLEY. went on leave to England. 7 men to England.	JWB.
	26.7.15		Resting.	JWB.
	27.7.15		Received orders to move tomorrow.	JWB.
LA GORGUE	28.7.15	7 a.m.	Battalion entrained in covered trucks. Regt & Serg-Major to Hospital sick after march to station.	JWB.
			Via MERVILLE, ST VENANT, ST OMER, HAZEBROUCK, CALAIS, BOULOGNE, ETAPLES, ABBEVILLE	
			(1 hour halt) to CORBIE. Detrained at 9.15 P.M. Billets good.	JWB.
CORBIE	29.7.15		In billets at CORBIE	JWB.
	30.7.15	1.30 P.M.	Marched out toward RIBEMONT 3.30 P.M. Inspected in Brigade by GEN. MUNRO Commanding 3rd Army. Arrived at ALBERT	JWB.
ALBERT	31.7.15	A.M.	arriving 10.45 P.M. after a march of 2½ hours.	JWB.
			C.O. and Adjutant visits Commander 2nd Rgt of d'Infantrie Francaise, whom we relieved in trenches, we	JWB.
			were still supported by French Artillery. 11.30 P.M. 3 men returned from Hospital.	JWB.

1577 Wt.W10791/1773 500,000 1/15 D.D. & L. A.D.S.S./Forms/C. 2118.

51st Division

2/5th Lancashire Fus.

Vol IV

From 1st to 31st Aug. 1915

121/6550

H.H.
13 sheets

WAR DIARY of 2/5 LANCASHIRE FUSILIERS.

or INTELLIGENCE SUMMARY.

Army Form C. 2118.

Place	Date	Hour	Summary of Events and Information	Remarks and references to Appendices
BOIS D'AUTHUILLE	1/8/15		Trenches well dug and clean, chiefly cut in chalk and clay. Two companies of 1/6th SCOTS RIFLES are in support. We were warned by French Intelly. Gloucester Officer that the enemy had cut his wire, and an attack is to be expected. Quiet night at 3 men rejoined from hospital. BRIGr GENl HIBBERT visited the trenches.	A/WD3
	2/8/15		Difficulty encountered in supply of water. Water cart fills at ALBERT and moves to BOIS D'AUTHUILLE four times daily. CAPT E R RAMSDEN reported to England — sick 22/7/15. 1 man to England 16/7/15, 1 man 18/7/15, 2 men 22/7/15, 4 men 25/7/15. MAJOR H. J. SHIRLEY returned from leave. 1 N.C.O. died in hospital of Enteric Fever.	A/WD3
	3/8/15		24/7/15. 3 men to Hospital - sick 31/7/15. 1 N.C.O September to Hosp. Sick 1/8/15. 2 men wounded.	A/WD3
	4/8/15	11.0 p.m.	Patrol of "Z" Coy under CAPT. HEDLEY, went out on left to stalk German working party. One man accidentally shot in shoulder. Minden Day congratulations from Depôt replied to. 1 man wounded. 1 to Hosp. sick (31/7/15) Band 1 man do. 4/8/15. One man returned from hospital 4/8/15. S-M-Crawford returned to duty 3/8/15. 4 platoons of 6th BERKS. REGt (R.A) distributed along line for instruction. LT-COL. DOWELL of above Regt visited trench with BRIG. GENl HIBBERT. Quiet day.	A/WD3
	5/8/15			

WAR DIARY
or
INTELLIGENCE SUMMARY.
(Erase heading not required.)

Army Form C. 2118.

Place	Date	Hour	Summary of Events and Information	Remarks and references to Appendices
	6.8.15		1 man killed, 1 wounded, and 1 BERKS. R & I man wounded by H-V. 77 m.m. shell. 1 man killed & one wounded 6.8.15. 2/LT K. WATERHOUSE and 8 N.C.O & men detailed to take the Trench Mortar Course from 9th inst.	AMB.
	7.8.15	8 p.m.	Two Three Companies less two platoons relieved by 1/5th SCOTS RIFLES.	
		9 p.m.	Two Companies less two platoons relieved by 1/4th LOYAL N. LANCS.	
			Dark night and great need out in mud. Batn in MARTINSART in very dirty billets. Batn in Divisional Reserve.	AMB.
MARTINSART	8.8.15	10.30a	Church Parade. Day spent cleaning billets, kit, etc. "W" Coy inlying picket.	AMB.
	9.8.15	11 a.m.	F.G.C.M. on 2496 Pte W. BRADLEY. 1 man to hospital – sick. "X" Coy Inlying Picket. 2 men from Hospital. 21 N.C.O's from to England.	AMB.
	10.8.15	11 a.m.	Reading of A.A. out-parma (f) & (g) and punishment laid down therein: 1 by inlying Picket. Promulgation of sentence on 2496 Pte W. BRADLEY. 58 days FP No 1. 9.38 days Pay for "Drunk at time of parade for Trenches 31/7/15". CAPT L.H.BLOY appointed acting Adjutant vice CAPT. J.W. JEFFREYS. Proceeding to rejoin his Battalion, the 6th DURHAM L.I.	AMB.
	11.8.15		CAPT. K.WATERHOUSE, and 9 N.C.O's sent on leave to England. CAPT JEFFREYS and 1 man	

WAR DIARY
or
INTELLIGENCE SUMMARY.
(Erase heading not required.)

Army Form C. 2118.

Instructions regarding War Diaries and Intelligence Summaries are contained in F. S. Regs., Part II. and the Staff Manual respectively. Title pages will be prepared in manuscript.

Place	Date	Hour	Summary of Events and Information	Remarks and references to Appendices
	12.8.15		returned to 1/6 D.L.I. 2 by Inlying Picket.	
			1 man from Hospital.	
		8.30 p.m	Battalion marched out to SENLIS, via BOUZINCOURT. Very bad roads & some rain falling. Some billets clean, others filthy. W by Inlying Picket.	
SENLIS.	13.8.15		# 1 N.C.O to Hospital. Two men rejoined from Hospital. 'X' by Inlying Picket	
	14.8.15		Resting & cleaning billets. 'X' by Inlying Picket. Marched to BOIS D'AUTHUILLE trenches and relieved L.N.L & S.R. at 8.15 p.m. Intended relieving at 9.30 p.m. but enemy balloon observed roads.	
	15.8.15		10 men to Hospital-sick. 1 man on special leave to England.	
	16.8.15		Quiet day, but much more lively than in previous visit to same trenches. Bursts of Machine Gun fire, together with H-V. 77 m.m shells, at night.	
	17.8.15		6 men to England. 3 men wounded, 4 men to Hospital sick.	
			CAPT. E.C. SIMON (wounded 16/8/15) died of wounds. 3 more men wounded. CAPT. SIMON had been working at evacuation of wounded lying and when returning was shot through the stomach.	
	18.8.15		5 men transferred to 178th Field Coy. R.E on the 19th inst. 5 men rejoined for duty	

WAR DIARY
or
INTELLIGENCE SUMMARY.
(Erase heading not required.)

Army Form C. 2118.

Place	Date	Hour	Summary of Events and Information	Remarks and references to Appendices
	10/8/15		2/Lt H WATERHOUSE & 8 N.C.O.s from attached 87th Trench Mortar Battery.	JMB.
	11/8/15		LT R W KIRKMAN invalided to England 11/8/15. 2 men wounded. 1 to hospital sick. 1 from hospital. All ranks on leave from 10.8.15 returned this day. 1 N.C.O. died of wounds.	JMB.
	20/8/15 21/8/15		Quiet day. Burst of M-G fire temporary all night. 1 shot of wounded killed, one to hospital sick. 4 men returned from hospital. 1 man wounded. 8 men on leave to England. 2 9 H.V. 77 mm shells in 20 mins over right corner of wood. Enemy machine guns busy. 1/4 K.R.R.C. comm. into support relieving 1/1 regt. sup? in their "X" coy. Mounted a machine gun emplacement of 77 m.m. gun by drawing fire and taking contour bearings of the flash. Their position was communicated to the Artillery, who replied on both points, and return did damage to their parapet, but failed to hit the gun. Late in the evening 2 men wounded.	JMB. JMB. JMB.
	23/8/15		LT C W B MILL to England 31/7/15; 2 men to England. 3 men wounded. Quiet day. 12th MIDDLESEX (K.A.) sent 2nd in command and 8 platoons for instruction. They were settled in the trenches by 9.30 pm when by prearranged	JMB.

WAR DIARY
or
INTELLIGENCE SUMMARY.

(Erase heading not required.)

Army Form C. 2118.

Place	Date	Hour	Summary of Events and Information	Remarks and references to Appendices
			signal with infantry, light guns bombarded new subs of the enemy. These had been located and working parties noted and fired on during the last few days. At 9.32 p.m. guns fired on junction of three saps and the enemy front trench, so as to catch the working parties as they returned.	
		9.45 p.m	The above having failed to draw on the enemy gun at 712, we endeavoured to draw their fire with our own M-Gs. from Plateforme emplacements, and swept the road used by enemy transport. We succeeded in drawing enemy fire. It was soon as it was fully established that the M.G. at 416 and the H-V 77 mm gun at 712 were occupying their old positions the heavy artillery opened fire on them. Their M-Gs opened again for a short time, but later all was quiet.	
			LT G.M. HUMBLE, LT S. COOPER, 2/LT T.M.O KUENDERDINE, 2/LT E.H. FRYER reported for duty. 3 men returned from Hospital, one from leave. MMS	
	24.X.15		Some slight shelling in morning. 2" Tm/s without movement either enemy scouts or enemy patrol in early morning, and had This men wounded.	

Army Form C. 2118.

WAR DIARY
or
INTELLIGENCE SUMMARY.
(Erase heading not required.)

Place	Date	Hour	Summary of Events and Information	Remarks and references to Appendices
	24.8.15		Much work has been done on parapets, furnaces, new traverses, communication trenches and sanitary arrangements. Dug-outs have been strengthened. First of all, we have pushed out our saps until they now reached the outer edge of our wire, in addition to this which have always been opened. Aug 24th one of our saps in X coy's line is known to the enemy who burnt a 77 mm shell over it at a listening post went out on the night of the 23rd inst. Enemy 77mm shells bursting round Battalion H-Q at intervals of 5 to 10 minutes. 14 shells in all. No damage done.	
		2 p.m.	About 2 hours enemy M.G. fire during night – otherwise quiet French work possible.	
		4 p.m.	4 shells (H-E) of larger calibre than usual fell in TRANCHÉE LANDAIS. Possibly 4"to 6". One traverse was damaged. Enemy fired Real Flares before artillery fire. Aspan flares fired between 9 and 11.15 p.m. Enemy sniper very active. 2/2E NOTON shot one through the chest during the morning.	

JWB.

WAR DIARY
or
INTELLIGENCE SUMMARY

Army Form C. 2118.

Place	Date	Hour	Summary of Events and Information	Remarks and references to Appendices
	26/2/15	1 a.m.	Sound of tractor pulling very heavy load along AUTHUILLE - OVILLERS road, near point 427. Patrols met no enemy. 3 men returned to duty. Suitable winter quarters ready for transport selected in BOUZINCOURT. On the whole a quiet day & night. About 12 N.E. 4"9" shells between 4 & 5 p.m, but in TRANCHÉES RAMAZOTTI and LAMAROUX, and 30 at all in and around TRANCHÉE RAGUET between 11 & 11.30 a.m. Result nil, except for slight damaging our parapet. Enemy snipers have found it best to adopt new positions and have been less active. Enemy working parties very busy again between 408 and 411, in and around 412, and about 425 - 426. We opened fire on this latter party at 12.30 a.m. and drove them in. CAPT HUTCHINSON and LIEUT. EVANS visited some shell holes and a low gully in which indication of tunnelling had been reported, but found all normal. Enemy's patrols not encountered and indeed do not seem willing (or allowed?) to come out lately. Enemy heard shouting and whistling in trench all day. At 4 a.m they called	

WAR DIARY
or
INTELLIGENCE SUMMARY
(Erase heading not required.)

Army Form C. 2118.

Place	Date	Hour	Summary of Events and Information	Remarks and references to Appendices
	26/9/17		out", "English good", "Slope arms", and "Have you any cigarettes"; "We want to go home." Weather very fine. No wiring in front of "X" Company, unlike the normal early mornings. "Y" Coy quiet so too, enabling us to do much work. Enemy still working at point 4.12. A large working party seen in front of our right company (i.e. in front of German points 4.26 - 4.27 - 4.28) reported to Capt. GOODSMITH in front of German points arranged for cross fire from SCOTTISH RIFLES M-G. For a time working ceased for cross fire. When it recommenced M-G opened again, and party withdrew. Enemy party retired to enemy trenches.

At 9.30 p.m. last night, standing patrol on the left reported two men approaching our position. One was killed, the other wounded & captured. A third man came up in rear of enemy patrol, but made good his escape. The wounded prisoner said the patrol consisted of two only. When patrol was captured enemy rockets were sent up & that enemy had been digging all day in front of our patrol at this point (point 4.11) Deceased soldier was under Officer W. ALBER 9/16 | |

Place	Date	Hour	Summary of Events and Information	Remarks and references to Appendices

1st at Regt. XIII Corps. He was killed partly by one of our shots, partly by the explosion of a bomb suspended round his neck. A live bomb was taken from the wounded prisoner. Great credit due to 2/Lt KEMP for his work in bringing in the two men, considering what his N.C.O. had a hysterical fit outside the parapet immediately after the capture. The N.C.O. was also brought in.

1 man accidentally wounded.

MAJOR T.D. BARNSDALE proceeded on leave to ENGLAND. 8 men go tomorrow. JWS

2/8/15
Day fairly quiet. Enemy fired 22 H.E. 77 mm shells into RAQUET between 11 a.m. & 1 p.m. Our own artillery in reply damaged enemy trenches and during the night stopped enemy working parties. Enemy had large working parties at 4.11, 4.12, 4.13, 4.15, and our patrols discovered it was impossible to get near them, as the enemy had a screen out. This screen followed our patrol in the region 4.B.4.14–4.15. That in front of 4.A.4.12 also advanced & fired at our trenches.

WAR DIARY
or
INTELLIGENCE SUMMARY.
(Erase heading not required.)

Army Form C. 2118.

Instructions regarding War Diaries and Intelligence Summaries are contained in F. S. Regs., Part II. and the Staff Manual respectively. Title pages will be prepared in manuscript.

Place	Date	Hour	Summary of Events and Information	Remarks and references to Appendices
	28.8.15		Working parties fired at + rifle grenades + M.G.s being opened on them. Noisy indicators of casualties were audible. Enemy was trying to join ends of their open new trench on ridge above our trenches. 1 man wounded. I rejoined from Hospital. Quiet day with few shells. Thunderstorm began at 7.30 p.m. "Z" Coy moved into support at POST DONNET, relieving a company of 1/4 KING'S OWN. (R.L.) REGT. W., X., + "Y" Coys relieved by 1/4 L.N.L. Rgt. & 7 + 2 Coys by 1/6 SCOTS RIFLES. Relief completed & Battalion in billets at AVELUY by 12.30 a.m.	J.M.B. J.M.B.
AVELUY	29.8.15		Church Parade of holy communion 11.15 a.m. Several shells fell in vicinity 1 man rejoined from Hospital. 1 killed at 4 p.m. Casualties N/Coys J.M.B.	
	30.8.15		"X" Coy working in FORT LOUIS and communication trench in JOIS D'AUTHUILLE. "Z" Coy returned from POST DONNET previous day in reserve to answering of due to presence of 12th MIDDLESEX in trenches for instruction. Shells on village near billets at 6 p.m.	J.M.B.
	31.8.15		Village shelled at 9 a.m. "Z" Coy returned to POST DONNET 11.15 p.m.	J.M.B.

WAR DIARY
or
INTELLIGENCE SUMMARY

Army Form C. 2118.

Place	Date	Hour	Summary of Events and Information	Remarks and references to Appendices
			CAPT. L.M. DLDY appointed Adjutant (Acting) from 11.8.15. dist No 44. Appt. Conmd approved by F.M. Comdg-in-Chief. dated 21.8.15.) 1 man wounded by shrapnel of falling in village 29-8-15. 1 man to Hospital sick. 1 man from Hospital.	AMB.

51st Division

12/690

2/5th Lancashire Fus'd

Cpl V

Sep 1. 15

Snell
S.H.
Hosheto

WAR DIARY
or
INTELLIGENCE SUMMARY

(Erase heading not required.)

Army Form C. 2118.

CONFIDENTIAL.

WAR DIARY

OF

2/5th BATT. LANCASHIRE FUSILIERS.

FROM. September 1. TO. September 30.

(VOLUME. 1.)

WAR DIARY of 2/5 Lanc. Fusiliers — Army Form C. 2118.

INTELLIGENCE SUMMARY.
(Erase heading not required.)

Place	Date	Hour	Summary of Events and Information	Remarks and references to Appendices
AVELUY.	1/9/15		In Bde. Reserve. 150 men working on BOYEAU BRUCE. One company, 2" buck at POST DONNET, support for Right Sector of Bde. 2/Lt T.C. LATTER left billet in AVELUY with 20 men permanent Bde. Fatigue Party. 100 men at Bomb School. 33 from "W", 33 from "X", 34 from "Y".	AWS.
	2/9/15		Lt HUMBLE, 2/Lt FRYER, 2/Lt YOUNG in charge of three parties for instruction. "Y" Company outlying picket. Same fatigue party at BOYEAU BRUCE. Same at Bomb School. 6 men reported to R.E. for Loading purposes near SENLIS. Returned at 10.p.m. Alarm at 10.5 p.m. as a test. Winton message to companies. "W" Company outlying picket, in position by 10.20 p.m. Whole battalion in position 10.55 p.m.	AWS. AWS.
	3/9/15	6.30pm	Some fatigue and working parties. "X" company outlying picket.	AWS.
	4/9/15	8.15pm	March to MARTINSART, to Divisional Reserve. Handed over billets to 1/8th K.L.R.	AWS.
	5/9/15	10.30am	Battalion in billets at MARTINSART. "Z" Company arrived 11.05 p.m. Church Parade.	AWS. AWS.

WAR DIARY
or
INTELLIGENCE SUMMARY.
(Erase heading not required.)

Army Form C. 2118.

Place	Date	Hour	Summary of Events and Information	Remarks and references to Appendices
MARTINSART	6/9/15		Working party 2 officers 150 N.C.O's & men at Bomb School at AVELUY. 100 N.C.O's & men in charge of Lt DUCKWORTH at m. Working party of 50 men for BDE. Began work on new Reservoir from.	AMS
"	7/9/15		Same working parties. Bomb School party billeted at AVELUY from Gh'y. One man wounded at Bomb School. N.C.O's drill class began. 2 N.C.O's wounded at this class by shrapnel.	JMS
"	8/9/15		Same working parties. Officers meeting 6 p.m. CAPT E.C. HUTCHINSON to take over duties of Adjutant. CAPT L.H. BLOY to command "Y" Coy vice CAPT G.C. HUTCHINSON. CAPT J.W. MEDLEY to command "W" Company vice CAPT G.H. GOLDSMITH, D.O.R.E.	JMS

WAR DIARY
INTELLIGENCE SUMMARY
(Erase heading not required.)

Army Form C. 2118.

Instructions regarding War Diaries and Intelligence Summaries are contained in F.S. Regs., Part II and the Staff Manual respectively. Title pages will be prepared in manuscript.

Hour, Date, Place	Summary of Events and Information	Remarks and references to Appendices
Martinsart. 9-9-15.	Battalion was in Divisional Res. Billets. Weaving Parties, strength 250, was provided as demanded by 154 Brigade. A Part. was employed requisitely in improving billets for unlit & conducting retention of N.C.O.'s. Mess reserve. Sight N.C.O.'s & men furnished as leave but were recalled by wiped message from 154's Bry. Bing. Casualties: 2376 Sgt Duckworth: to Arty. Emp. Sergt. Maj. Strength: Rifles. 614. Total. 671. Wealth; Sighw. 6.	C.C.11
Martinsart. 10-9-15.	Batt. relieved 1/6 Scottish Rifles & 1/4 L.N.LAN. REGT. in F2 sector in front of AUTHILLE & BOIS D'AUTHILLE. Enemy shelled junction of centre Coys. Two casualties were sustained in o/R. Total 2R. Strength: Rifles. 600.	C.C.11
Post Lesboeufs, Authille. 11-9-15.	Extract from B.O. "SAA: Coy. were on duty in trenches will be supplied with trench kits; all ammunition expended will be taken from Unit bandaliers & has been ammunition & transferred in trenches; Coys will daily maintain to trenches.	

Army Form C. 2118.

WAR DIARY
or
INTELLIGENCE SUMMARY.
(Erase heading not required.)

Instructions regarding War Diaries and Intelligence Summaries are contained in F.S. Regs., Part II. and the Staff Manual respectively. Title pages will be prepared in manuscript.

Hour, Date, Place	Summary of Events and Information	Remarks and references to Appendices
POST LESBOEUFS, AUTHUILLE 13-9-16	No incidents. Front seemingly to be expected in. Trench manners anything. Strength: Rifles. 608; Total. 810. Strength: Rifles. 612. Total. 810.	B.O.6. 12/9/16. C.C.H. C.C.H.
POST LESBOEUFS, AUTHUILLE 13-9-16	Incidents nil. Quiet in front of Z Coy. L. Sector. 2961 Pte CHADWICK was killed in firing bay by enemy sniper. Body 26230 L/Cpl BURGON was wounded by enemy sniper. At night time was spent by M. Guns in covering sapheads of front. R. centre Coy: enemy refills will Blackpool. A 3691 Pte MARTIN was wounded. Strength: Rifles. 608. Total 604.	C.C.H.
POST LESBOEUFS, AUTHUILLE 14-9-16	Strength: Rifles 609. Total. 600.	C.C.H.
POST LESBOEUFS, AUTHUILLE 15-9-16	Strength: Rifles. 611. Total. 800.	C.C.H.

Army Form C. 2118.

WAR DIARY
or
INTELLIGENCE SUMMARY

(Erase heading not required.)

Hour, Date, Place	Summary of Events and Information	Remarks and references to Appendices
POST LES DOS, AUTHUILE 16-9-15	Information was received from Brig.-Maj., 151st Inf. Brig. that a sufficiency of Frenchmen were in the officers' & men's quarters in Sgt. Ball's sector & that Staffin soldiers & arrived there & will be following under orders: "Officers & O.R. belonging to visit the late of 151st Inf. Brig. will be stopped and sent under an Frenchmen of Trenches will be taken to O.C. Coy Trooping Sentry who will answer to him to be found to obey this order." Strength: Rifles: 610. Total: 795.	B.O.B. 16-9-15 C.C.N.
POST LES DOS, AUTHUILE 17-9-15	Strength: Rifles: 608. Total: 794.	C.C.N.
POST LES DOS, AUTHUILE 18-9-15	Strength: Rifles: 607. Total: 794.	C.C.N.

WAR DIARY or INTELLIGENCE SUMMARY

Army Form C. 2118.

Hour, Date, Place	Summary of Events and Information	Remarks and references to Appendices
POST LES DOS. AUTHUILLE 19-9-15.	Strength. Rifles 603 Total. 794.	C.E.H.
POST LES DOS. AUTHUILLE 20-9-15.	Strength. Rifles. 604 Total 794.	C.E.H.
POST LES DOS. AUTHUILLE 21-9-15.	Battalion was relieved in Fr. sect by 1/5 Sea. Highrs. Battalion returned to rest billets at SENLIS to refitting & carrying out programme of training. 2701 Pte. LAMB accidentally wounded by rifle bullet. Total. 794. Strength: Rifles. 600	C.E.H.
SENLIS, 22-9-15.	Coys. refitted boots & clothing & carried out daily Programme Physical training. A board of enquiry assembled to investigate circumstances attending wounding of 2701 Pte. LAMB : Board found evidence of self-inflicted wound; Hundrug adduced was insufficient evidence to send case by S.I.S. Div.	

WAR DIARY
or
INTELLIGENCE SUMMARY

(Erase heading not required.)

Army Form C. 2118.

Hour, Date, Place	Summary of Events and Information	Remarks and references to Appendices
SENLIS. 28-9-15.	Lieut. M. HALL. Leave and duties of S. in L. recent of 2 Coy. Strength. 600. Total. 794.	C.E.N.
	Programme of training continued; Bomb convoies; Close order Drill, Physical drill, extending from artillery formations. Strength, 602. Total, 791.	C.E.N.
SENLIS. 24-9-15.	Programme as 23-9-15. continued. Strength, Rifles. 597. Total. 777.	C.E.N.
SENLIS, 25-9-15.	Batt. carried out route march; Route following:– SENLIS, HERAUVILLE, FORCEVILLE, ACHEUX, VARENNES, SENLIS. There were no march casualties; Weather rain during greater part of day. Strength; Rifles: 595. Total. 775.	C.E.N.

Army Form C. 2118.

WAR DIARY
or
INTELLIGENCE SUMMARY.
(Erase heading not required.)

Instructions regarding War Diaries and Intelligence Summaries are contained in F. S. Regs., Part II. and the Staff Manual respectively. Title pages will be prepared in manuscript.

Hour, Date, Place	Summary of Events and Information	Remarks and references to Appendices
SENLIS, 26-9-16.	Batt. relieved 1/5: SEA. HIGHLDS. & 1/6 SEA. HIGHLDS. less 14 platoons in F2 sector in front of AUTHUILE a Bois D' AUTHUILE: Batt. left SENLIS 6.15 reached AVELUY at 6.15 & Post LES BOIS 7.30: relief was complete at 8.30. Weather: Heavy rain all day & during relief. Strength: Rifles . 569 Total 776.	C.C.M.

1247 W 3299 200,000 (E) 8/14 J.B.C. & A. Forms/C. 2118/11.

Army Form C. 2118.

WAR DIARY
or
INTELLIGENCE SUMMARY
(Erase heading not required.)

Hour, Date, Place	Summary of Events and Information	Remarks and references to Appendices
AVELUY 9.30 p.m. 27-9-18.	Automatic cannon district of PERONNE, BAPAUME, were received from 151st Inf. Bgde. Two Lewis Gun teams were drawn from right of F2 sector every night till 7 a.m. Shells, wounding on Corporal 1/6 L'POOL REGT. Strengths: Rifles: 589. Total: 776. Weather: Raining; trenches extremely dirty.	E.L.

WAR DIARY
or
INTELLIGENCE SUMMARY
(Erase heading not required.)

Army Form C. 2118.

Instructions regarding War Diaries and Intelligence Summaries are contained in F. S. Regs, Part II. and the Staff Manual respectively. Title pages will be prepared in manuscript.

Hour, Date, Place	Summary of Events and Information	Remarks and references to Appendices
AVELUY. 28-9-15. 9.30.	Working Parties in trenches & Support trenches were renewed. No Sap in B/4 catr. B/4 was deepened on A/4 front. K.2 was deepened on A/4 House L dug. Casualties: 1 O.R. Killed. 1 Rifleman with Fire Control wounded. 1 O.R. 586 Tml. Rifles. Strength: Rifles Weather: Showers all day, trenches very muddy, movement difficult.	
AVELUY. 29-9-15. 9.30 p.m.	Work in trenches was again carried on. Suspicions with regard had been entertained on previous days of enemy's lines being stocked up & troops withdrawn were dispelled as large parties of Germans were observed in various places & individuals at front in German lines. News was received of fierce attacks & British victories in CHAMPAGNE & hier hors. Streett Rifles. Total 778 Weather: Steady rain. Forms/C.2118/II.	C.C.!!

Army Form C. 2118.

WAR DIARY
or
INTELLIGENCE SUMMARY
(Erase heading not required.)

Instructions regarding War Diaries and Intelligence Summaries are contained in F. S. Regs., Part II. and the Staff Manual respectively. Title pages will be prepared in manuscript.

Hour, Date, Place	Summary of Events and Information	Remarks and references to Appendices
AVELUY. 30/9/18 9.30 p.m.	Trench work was again resumed. Germans were observed about 6.30 p.m. advancing though enemy barrage violent. No signs of weakening of German line was evident. Enemy troops having position carrying stores, rations, men & horses were again observed. No hostile shells of nature N. of line was received. Shelling: Rifles 576. Trench: 770. Casualties: 1 officer (Lieut. Jones) accidentally injured in hand on entanglement. Other ranks still very muddy & movement difficult. Weather: No rain; trenches still very muddy & movement difficult.	C.C.?!

51st Division

2/5th Lancs. Fus.

Oct 1915

Vol VI

Army Form C. 2118.

WAR DIARY
or
INTELLIGENCE SUMMARY.
(Erase heading not required.)

CONFIDENTIAL

WAR DIARY.

OF.

2/5. BATT. LANCASHIRE FUSILIERS.

FROM. OCTOBER 31 1915. TO OCTOBER 31 1915.

VOLUME 1.

[Stamp: 6TH BATT* LANCASHIRE FUSILIERS, Date 1/X/15, No. ___]

Army Form C. 2118.

WAR DIARY
or
INTELLIGENCE SUMMARY

(Erase heading not required.)

Instructions regarding War Diaries and Intelligence Summaries are contained in F. S. Regs., Part II. and the Staff Manual respectively. Title pages will be prepared in manuscript.

Hour, Date, Place	Summary of Events and Information	Remarks and references to Appendices
AVELUY. 1-10-15 9.30 p.m.	Usual wire in support & for Vickers were continued. Brig. General C.L. HIBBERT D.S.O. cmdg. 138th Inf. Bde. was wounded in shoulder at POST LESDOS, whilst visiting Battn. Weather: Bright all day, mud & water in trenches was considerably reduced. Strength: Rifles 567 Total: 784. Casualties: Nil.	
AVELUY. 2-10-15 9.30 p.m.	Usual wire in support & for Vickers were carried on. Weather: Bright, mud etc in trenches considerably reduced. Strength: Rifles 561 Total 783. Casualties: Died of wounds. 3047 Pte. MITCHEL "X" Coy.	C.C.H
AVELUY. 3-10-15 4.50.	Batt. were relieved in fire trenches by 1/6 Sea. Rif. & 1/4 L.N.Lanc. regt. Batt. less 1 Coy proceeded in Brig. Res. an POST AVELUY (village) Y. Coy proceeded into support an POST DONNET.	C.C.H

1247 W 8299 200,000 (E) 8/14 J.B.C. & A. Forms/C. 2118/11.

WAR DIARY
or
INTELLIGENCE SUMMARY
(Erase heading not required.)

Army Form C. 2118.

Hour, Date, Place	Summary of Events and Information	Remarks and references to Appendices
AVELUY (billets)	Batt. lines were inspected by Maj. Gen. G.T. HARPER, G.O.C. 51st Divn. Weather: Bright all day. Strength: Rifles 561. Total 763. Casualties: accidentally wounded 1 O.R.	C.C.H
AVELUY. 4-10-15	Batt. in Brigade reserve: Duties were found as follows:— i. b/ Post DONNET, 1 Coy in support. ii. at AVELUY, 1 Coy helping Pioneers; providing 4 Cookers & 2 Swank Guards. iii. 1 Coy providing Working Fatigue, in subsects. 140-144; 1/ 2 Coy unloading stuff & in from Henri Shifflo iv. ay Post DONNET. 20 men = 1 off. v. ay AVELUY (R.E. store) 10 O.R. vi. ay AVELUY Signals, & O.R. Duties (iii)-(vi) interchanged between Coys. Strength: Rifles 560 Total: 763. Weather: Wet; cold.	

Army Form C. 2118.

WAR DIARY
or
INTELLIGENCE SUMMARY

(Erase heading not required.)

Instructions regarding War Diaries and Intelligence Summaries are contained in F. S. Regs., Part II. and the Staff Manual respectively. Title pages will be prepared in manuscript.

Hour, Date, Place	Summary of Events and Information	Remarks and references to Appendices
AVELUY. 5-10-'15.	Same parties were furnished as 4-10-15. Strength Rifles 674 Total 771. Weather: Bright cold.	C.C.11
AVELUY. 6-10-15.	Same parties furnished as 5-10-15. Strength: Rifles. 574 Total 771. Casualties: 2nd Lieut. Evans very slightly wounded by shrapnel: did not leave duty.	C.C.11
AVELUY. 7-10-15.	Same parties were furnished as 6-10-15. Strength: Rifles. 571. Total 771. Casualties. 1 O.R. wounded by shell fire in trenches. Draft. 11 O.R. from Base.	C.C.11
AVELUY. 8-10-15	Same parties continued furnished as 6-10-15. Strength. Rifles. 567 Total 769. 1 Coy was relieved by 1 Coy 1/6 Liverpool Regt on POST DONNET & proceeded to Bois Riaumont.	C.C.11

WAR DIARY
or
INTELLIGENCE SUMMARY

(Erase heading not required.)

Army Form C. 2118.

Hour, Date, Place	Summary of Events and Information	Remarks and references to Appendices
AVELUY. 9-10-15 6 p.m.	Following parties were furnished:— 1/ 1 off. 10 O.R. Rejoining in AVELUY. 2/ 1 off. 10 O.R. Tunnelling. (Relief any 4 hours 8.30 a.m. 8.30 p.m.) 3/ 1 off. 8 O.R. R.E. stores AVELUY. 4/ 1 off. 300 O.R. Signals. 5/ 1 off. 10 O.R. Rock St. 6/ 1 off. 30 O.R. Railway to HESCOS. 7/ 2 off. 50 O.R. Tram line Ft Sentry. 8/ 1 off. 20 O.R. down o' GAUNT ST. Strength: Rifles: 565, Total, 753. Wounded: (old) evacuated.	C.e.11

WAR DIARY
or
INTELLIGENCE SUMMARY

(Erase heading not required.)

Army Form C. 2118.

Hour, Date, Place	Summary of Events and Information	Remarks and references to Appendices
AVELUY 10/10/15. 9.30.	Same routine was provided on 9/10/15. Battalion were only just able to furnish the usual parties owing to large guards, Bath school etc. A requisitioned Bank School were founded under C. Sergt. Kenefick; 2 N.C.O.'s to attend and all serjeants engaged to attend a course. Strength: Rifles; 565 — Total: 751	E.E.H
AVELUY. 11/10/15 5 pm	Same routine was carried out on 10/10/15. W.O.'s & C.Q.M.S.s examined by Lt. Col. R. T. EDWARDS under 15th Army List Rules. Strength; 325 Total: 752	E.T.E

WAR DIARY or INTELLIGENCE SUMMARY

Army Form C. 2118.

Hour, Date, Place	Summary of Events and Information	Remarks and references to Appendices
POST NR AVELUY. 12/X/15.	Same wandering Posts as were found on 11/X/15. Strength: Rifles 561. Total 748.	L.C.II
AVELUY. 13/X/15.	Same wandering Parties were found as 12/X/15. Strength: Rifles 557. Total 747. Casualties: 1 O.R. wounded by shrapnel.	L.C.II
AVELUY. 14/X/15.	Same wandering Parties were furnished as 13/X/15. A shell fell in cook house of 'Y' during issue of the rations & killing orderly Sergeant (Sgt. Kay) & 1 cook (Ricketts) & wounding 2 O.R. men. Strength: Rifles 550. Total 744. Casualties: 2 O.R. killed, 2 O.R. wounded.	L.C.II
POST LES BOIS. 15/X/15.	Battn. which relieved 1/6 Sco. Rif. & 1/4 L.N.L. Regt. in Fr. Scales at 1.30 p.m. 1 Officer & 7 O.R. proceeded to England on leave. Strength: Rifles 545. Total 743.	L.C.II

WAR DIARY
or
INTELLIGENCE SUMMARY

(Erase heading not required.)

Army Form C. 2118.

Hour, Date, Place	Summary of Events and Information	Remarks and references to Appendices
POST LESBOS. 16/X/15	Batt. was in occupation of front line Kereleos. The whole of since has been increasing activity; complaints of infantry in intermittent following enemy were received from 18th Inf. Bde. "Considerable movements of troops are reported east of us; this may indicate hostile intentions against front of Third Army; anyone that owners new reserves in to be existing schemes of defence & submit simple plans of your immediate action in event of attack." Strength: Rifles 534. Total 737.	C.L.H.
POST LESBOS. 17/X/15	S.A. NOTON a machinist Pabel Shor a gunner in enemy transport at 5.30 a.m. Enemy taking very active interest from dif. sorts of places & continue shooting up. Strength: Rifles 520 Total 735.	

WAR DIARY
or
INTELLIGENCE SUMMARY

(Erase heading not required.)

Army Form C. 2118.

Instructions regarding War Diaries and Intelligence Summaries are contained in F. S. Regs., Part II. and the Staff Manual respectively. Title pages will be prepared in manuscript.

Hour, Date, Place	Summary of Events and Information	Remarks and references to Appendices
POST LESDOS. 18/X/15.	Enemy was reported by my Snipers. A Gunner was observed working in Arras near 406. Strength: Rifles 528. Total, 734.	C.C.H.
POST LESDOS. 19/X/15.	Brigade reported that an enemy relief was affected. No information confirming this was obtained. Strength: Rifles 524 Total 726. Casualties: 2 O.R. wounded.	C.C.H.
POST LESDOS. 20/X/15.	Enemy heavily bombarded Subs, Scales. 140–142. held 1½ × Coy with 4.7", 6.5.8", 77mm shells a heavy trench mortar; considerable damage was done to trench & wire entanglements, organised retaliation was slightly directed. Strength: 515 Total 726. Casualties: 10.R. wounded. Weather: Very wet.	C.C.H.

Army Form C. 2118.

WAR DIARY
or
INTELLIGENCE SUMMARY

(Erase heading not required.)

Instructions regarding War Diaries and Intelligence Summaries are contained in F.S. Regs., Part II. and the Staff Manual respectively. Title pages will be prepared in manuscript.

Hour, Date, Place	Summary of Events and Information	Remarks and references to Appendices
LESDOS. 21/X/15.	Posta unchanged. Strength; Rifles 40 504. Total; 726. Weather; Very cold.	A.C.11
LESDOS. 22/X/15.	Situation unchanged. Strength; Rifles 497. Total 723.	A.C.11
LESDOS. 23/X/15.	Situation unchanged. Strength; Rifles 497. Total 714. Weather; cold as well.	A.C.11
LESDOS. 24/X/15	Situation unchanged. 1 O.R. wounded whilst working in advanced sap. Strength; Rifles 497. Total. 714. Casualties. 1 O.R. wounded.	A.C.11
LESDOS; 25/X/15.	Situation unchanged. Strength, Rifles 497; Total. 792.	A.C.11
LESDOS; 26/X/15;	Situation unchanged. Strength, Rifles 491. Total. 789.	A.C.11

Army Form C. 2118.

WAR DIARY
or
INTELLIGENCE SUMMARY

(Erase heading not required.)

Instructions regarding War Diaries and Intelligence Summaries are contained in F. S. Regs., Part II. and the Staff Manual respectively. Title pages will be prepared in manuscript.

Hour, Date, Place	Summary of Events and Information	Remarks and references to Appendices
AVELUY. 27/X/15.	Batt. were relieved by 1/4 L.N.L. REGT. & 1/5 Sco. RIF. of 3.30 p.m.: Batt. less A & B Coy proceeded to Bivouac. Remained in AVELUY: 1 Coy attached to Coy 1/4 K.O.R. LANCS. REGT. in POST BONNET. Strength inf/o 491 Total 730.	C.C./A
AVELUY. 28/X/15.	Fatigue Parties of 246 men were found for work on trenches: an average of 16 o.R. a.ssumed from Infantry Base Depot. Strength: Officers 586. Other Ranks 720.	C.C./A
AVELUY 29/X/15	Fatigue parties of 246 found for work on front line trenches Strength Rifles 493 Total 719 Casualties 2 Lieut J.W. Harker very slightly wounded by trench mortar. 2 O R wounded	J.S.
AVELUY 30/X/15	Fatigue parties of 246 found Strength Rifles 489 Total 719	J.S.

WAR DIARY
or
INTELLIGENCE SUMMARY.
(Erase heading not required.)

Army Form C. 2118.

Hour, Date, Place	Summary of Events and Information	Remarks and references to Appendices
AVELUY 31-X-15	Fatigue Parties of 246 found for front line trenches. During night of 30th a bombardment of AVELUY took place; commencing about 9 P.m. the bomb- ment continued until about 3 a.m. the following morning; in all about 120 shells of various sizes from 6.2 to 77 mm fell in village. Shrapnel 479 Total 716. Casualties sustained during bombardment Killed: 2318 Cpl. BIRTWHISTLE E. 8087 Pte TODD. W. Wounded: G. O. R.	G.G.

www.ingramcontent.com/pod-product-compliance
Lightning Source LLC
Chambersburg PA
CBHW081454160426
43193CB00013B/2474